Well Disposed

Gary Coles

MERMERUS BOOKS
AUSTRALIA

The author can be contacted via

sales @bookpod.com.au

First published in 2022

ISBN: 978-1-922270-85-6

Books by Gary Coles

Very Much So
The Lure of the Trail
Coming out of the Lockdown

Ever After: Fathers and the Impact of Adoption
Transparent: Seeing Through the Legacy of Adoption
The Invisible Men of Adoption
Made in Australia: The Adoption Apologies
Disturbing Adoption: The Collected Pieces

DEDICATION

To Aaron, Emerson, Sebastian and August, my grandchildren; because of the pandemic I could barely visit them during 2020 and 2021

Preamble

For much of 2020, Victoria, Australia was in lockdown. Confined to home but intent on staying connected I took on a writing project, which spread over several months. In September alone I wrote a poem a day, many of which appear in this compilation within the section called *2020 Visions*.

By 2021, COVID-19 lockdown fatigue had set in and I was less productive. Twenty-three contributions appear here under *The Ripple Effect*.

In 2022, for the sake of completion I have included a few poems from my previous books *Very Much So* and *The Lure of the Trail*, set behind *The Way Ahead*.

The waves emanating from these three years appear on the cover.

Overall and essentially, I set out to avoid writing pretentious poetry. On the way, I had fun with words.

There are good reasons for sharing per verse:

The essence

Whilst many have discovered
The passing joys of writing verse
Further rewards brood within
Set your effort to concentrate
On what moves to be said
And arrive well disposed
To reveal the sum of your truth.

Word imagery and rhyme
Can help the poet focus
On what is most important
That you hope to convey
Memorably and with elan
You aim to hit a chord
Where you are being read.

Verse the ready means to probe
What makes us thrive or slow
About what engages irks pleases
Or distresses us so we find
The rhythms of life and word
Lie at the very heart
Of what it means to be.

CONTENTS

The Way Ahead

What COVID-19 meant . . .

I'm not talking to myself, I'm having a parent-teacher conference!

My mum always told me I wouldn't accomplish anything by lying in bed all day. But look at me now! I'm saving the world!

My husband purchased a world map and then gave me a dart and said, "Throw this and wherever it lands – that's where I'm taking you when this pandemic ends." Turns out, we're spending two weeks behind the fridge!

All ex **The Scotsman**, 15th January 2021

2020 Visions

This incident had the potential to derail a trip to South America, soon after it began

How to avoid going shopping in Buenos Aires

First listen to your knowing partner
Where the best shops are to be found
Get close to where they start to flourish
And then . . . fall over on the ground

The ingredients are a bollard and
Multitasking so it has to be this male
Looking for a sign and also at a map
Thus on my sturdy glasses I did impale

My head it hit the footpath hard
And the gashes they began to gush

Well Disposed

My brow and nose took the brunt
Of my body plummeting full flush

Locals came running they had a chair
Some paper towels and soothing water
The sign language they all used said
So much blood suggests a slaughter

Someone there summoned the police
Who were shortly after to arrive
They called an ambulance unbidden
Hell would my hip pocket survive?

We wailed our way out to La Boca
For Emergencia we did not have to ask
But to find a doctor who understood us
Proved a somewhat lengthy task

Eventually there arrived a surgeon *

Whose basic English was the key
"You must not look notorious"
Was her departure goal for me

Into my forehead she sewed eight stitches
X-ray scans were necessary after that
To make sure my nose was unbroken
And all because I had gone splat

At the finish I looked a pretty sight
Gauze and tape plastered across my face
They said we could leave the hospital
But of a bill there was no trace

Then we found out the awesome secret
Argentina has medical services at no cost
Whereas Chile charges its patients
Luckily the border we had crossed

Well Disposed

Next day we flew south to Patagonia
The airline thought I'd been bashed
I told them the truth about my accident
How on to the pavement I had crashed

The stitches came out in Ushuaia
The last stop before a Chilean cruise
On the advice of my La Boca doctor
Argentina the place you have to choose

So if you want to avoid going shopping
And pesky bollards are your pick
Make sure you time your impact
For where it is free to get sick

Or better still don't be so drastic
Just to save a credit card or two
After all a little heady shopping
Should not hurt either me or you.

* *Thank you, Dr Lucila Brana*

The mountain spine of South America has a lot to offer

Along the mighty Andes

Fair Chile and Argentina lie
Side by side along the Andes
More than four thousand clicks
It's where majestic condors fly

And road and rail scarcely succeed
Via many tarmac switchbacks or
Narrow gauges that have to use the cog
To cross the high passes at low speed

In winter these routes may be closed
As snow and ice come into play
Often for several days at a time
Thus the fragile links are exposed.

Well Disposed

In the far south of the mountain chain
The westerly winds are a constant
And the clouds are forever shaping
Which means abundant falls of rain

So home to huge plateaus of ice
That grind down the slopes as glaciers
Not in retreat like most of their kind
Indeed some in to the sea they slice.

However in the north it is really sere
For the Atacama downfall is spasmodic
Rain shadows cast from east and west
Means moisture rarely makes it here
The landscape is flamboyant and stark
With a desert palette of earthy colours
Against a backdrop of volcanoes galore
Stargazers are in heaven after it gets dark.

Well Disposed

Now and then downpours cause a flood
Where in the absence of any vegetation
The soaking liquefies the fragile soil
And communities are engulfed by mud.

Overall such catastrophes are rare
All the better for we southern travellers
To visit ponder and very much admire
What the mighty Andes have to share.

This is autobiographical, capturing an episode that changed my life and the lives of two other people; it was written before Kay died in 2020

The family to be

A long time ago, several decades past,
When an adolescent in my family,
Where sex was never to be raised,
Uncertain of myself and the world.
Naive, self still forging an identity,
Looking for love and love looking for me.

Serendipity – finding and sharing love
Profound, passionate, compassionate.
A life together – forever – the dream,
The plan, but wait, studies to complete
Before two can become the one,
For Kay, my first love and me.

Well Disposed

Both twenty, powerful feelings
We become carried away so …
Now a child to come early.
Our plans brought forward,
Big hurdles to confront.
A pregnancy before marriage
What will both our parents say?
Kay cannot share her secret
And I fail to find an answer
When called upon to provide.

Overwhelmed I withdraw my support.
Agony for Kay – she goes away from home.

A hasty decision taken our love goes forsaken,
She is left holding my commitment undone.

I am ashamed; we share letters and I wait

For news of a baby born in another town.
She names her son after me the absent father.
Taken from his mother both so distraught,
As strangers adopt Kay's infant wailing boy,
Handy I grip denial for twenty years and more.

Could we have made it, before as a couple
Then kept a family after the birth of our son?
Through the lens of maturity we do come to see
Marriage had been possible, our family intact,
With common courage, panic then foregone,
Considerate decisions, the stigmas overcome.

Love found and lost, but never forgotten.
Our separate marriages yet parallel lives
Each blessed with further children
Shadowed by barely spoken regret
For the bonds created and broken
And our family that was not to be.

Well Disposed

May our son know and accept the love
We joyfully gave to his conception.
May his life be blessed with wisdom
Growth and the certainty of knowing
That behind the sorrow and the pain
Of separation are two caring people
Waiting ready always to embrace
We three the family that is yet to be.

A short exploration of a troubling phenomenon – our propensity to be swayed by opinion, not to act on facts

Blindness

Why does unreason often hold sway
Over evidence traced to sound data?
Harking appeals to fear and anger
Rears the certainty of being misled
Sooner led by pause and consider
Trumps to trusting the truth.

I was moved by a description I read in a novel set in Central Otago, New Zealand

Contentment

The trembling of the poplar leaves
Golden clusters shimmy in the breeze
Sure sign of autumn easing summer away
Warmth is evaporating seeing out the day
It's the change of seasons I so want to stay.

The conjunction between nature and numbers has always intrigued me

Fibonacci

Look deep into nature
Fibonacci holds the key
Count the petals on a rose
The spirals in a sunflower
Actually going both ways
The arrangement of leaves
On the stem of a plant
The spots fanning out
On the peacock's tail
All follow the equation
Of Fn = Fn-2 + Fn-1
Where n is 2 or more
Go make sense of that. *

* all 13 lines, a Fibonacci number

The trigger for this poem was the untimely death of the daughter of dear friends

In their prime

Death is a certainty but death can be unkind
Young lives ended people taken in their prime
Lost before their parents just not meant to go
Unnatural precedence impossible to foreknow
Natural the grieving for what should have been
Oh the heartache of young deaths unforeseen.

A call for considerateness during the pandemic

It has to be the sea you see

[a timely reminder of what John Donne wrote: 'No man is an island entire of itself']

Islands we are not for in an endless sea
Truly we are connected by our humanity

As this pandemic we seek to outsmart
We need be together by keeping apart

Call to stop the spread of personal emissions
This is no place for maverick positions

Follow the advice of those who know best
The facts not the rantings of the obsessed

Potential droplets exhaled on every breath

Well Disposed

We all bear an obligation to forestall death

Social distancing and out wearing a mask
Mutual benefits surely not too much to ask

If united we are to conquer this our calamity
We must act not as islands but truly the sea.

This is a lament for the demise of sound journalism

Misguided

What is it that we have done so very wrong
To deserve reportage of lurid distraction
Beset by tragedy conflict and sensation
Disclosure gossip more vacuous persuasion
When well informed is where we aim to belong?

I was inspired by a documentary about this famous locomotive

Ode to the *Flying Scotsman*

Hail the *Flying Scotsman*
The steam locomotive sublime
Forever the pride of British railways
Expressly on the north eastern line

Record the *Flying Scotsman*
On top for distance and for speed
On time too another hallmark
Gresley rightly proud of his steed

Retired the *Flying Scotsman*
Running in countries overseas
Canada, the US and downunder

Where the throngs it did please

Preserve the *Flying Scotsman*
For we have steam in our veins
Keep her splendid on the tracks
Steaming at the head of trains.

Another documentary on television caused me to write this tribute

Testament

Dame Elisabeth Murdoch noble in name and deed
Philanthropy and kindness at the centre of her creed
Splendid Cruden Gardens a measure of her open heart
Where design and verve and colour create a world apart
So well she brings us together, to meet a very human need.

A celebration of the change of season, which in 2020 seemed more significant because it occurred during the lockdown

The glories of spring

Jonquils and daffodils waving across the grass
Spring is coming means winter soon will pass
Prepare to be awakened nature on full display
More buds due to open on every passing day

Orchards in full blossom a riot of exquisite hues
Hail a fruitful season which one will you choose
Over the ornamental cherry on your front lawn
Bright pink short-lived and so delicate in form

A finely pruned rose is a blessing in disguise
Dormant before the blooms acclaim paradise
Then a riot of colour and fragrance to delight

Pleasure to the senses the crowning spring rite

Just a few of the pleasures for this time of year
Pause then absorb the wonder while you are here.

*The trigger here was an online article by Jessica Martin, **'Tiny wonders helped me through depression'***

The little things are the big things (out there)

Lockdown under COVID-19
Means outside is restricted
But yet not totally off limits

So go beyond wander and absorb
Pause to focus on and notice
The wonders that are out there
Time to listen to the magpies
Quardling on your front lawn.
To rest smell the flowers
Admire the bees at work
Find the pleasure in man and dog

Undivided cavorting with a ball
And see again vibrant colours
Drained pale with you indoors.

Once you have focussed on the awe
Within the little things out there
Then time to reflect and home in
On what has sustained you truly
Truly the big things out there.

Wonderment at another miracle of nature

The Phoenix tree

The amazing eucalyptus
Takes fire to survive
After being burned
It rises from the ashes
Reborn, the phoenix tree.

Decades of observing my surrounds and frustrations over the lack of progress dealing with the impacts of climate change is the impetus here. The lessons learned in Victoria, where, in 2020 people co-operated to stem the pandemic does, however, offer a ray of hope

Nature without reserve

It is nature I most of all revere
Sharing the wonders of symbiosis
Bestride a pinnacle with osmosis
Wondrous things within our sphere

The acknowledgement of beauty
Is what causes me to respond
To that I feel and more beyond
There is the call of human duty
To acclaim and also to preserve
Nature's glories so far bestowed

Well Disposed

Neither to plunder nor to erode
This the bounty we should serve

But plenty of us are so engrossed
In what is going on round about
Ourselves is what we most act out
'I look after number one' the boast

So is it little wonder that I pause
To chastise the impact of mankind
The quest for domination blind
To the casualties that we cause
Not only to this Earth which is our home
But also mutual regard risks to be undone
If we choose to avoid discourse one on one
Tragic our selfishness the rife syndrome

Our generation the one with the distinction
Through felling forests and staking land

Well Disposed

Watching fertile fields become drifts of sand
Of presiding over global mass extinction
Animals and plants killed as we spread
The atmosphere unclean emission heated
Abundant evidence of a planet maltreated
While human expansion pushes on ahead

True my faith in people has fallen through
For there are many problems to be solved
Where facts are surely best to be involved
Yet overwhelmed by spurious points of view
Opinions spin-doctored as if they are true
An uninformed few try to hijack the chore
So then emerging from the lack of rapport
More disillusionment is bound to ensue

Sadly I am drawn to be a misanthrope
Small talk that filler often bothers me
Wide discussion instead my constant plea

Well Disposed

I eschew superficiality of numbing scope
It is people who are at the core of trouble
Anthropocentric vanity our common blight
Homo sapiens obliged to assert their might
Stop surely time to look outside our bubble

To the marvels that exist if we care to look
Red Sea coral brilliant beneath the waves
The sightless fish deep inside dark caves
The pure clean water of a tinkling brook
Aurora borealis curtains the clear northern skies
Moved by canny chameleon matching its surrounds
Coned Tanna volcano erupting to explosive sounds
Best we do respond to our heart our ears and eyes

We are known in the past to have soared
Witness Angkor Wat and the pyramids at Giza
The tribute Taj Mahal enigmatic Mona Lisa
Where curiosity and creativity are in accord

Well Disposed

Fibonacci patterns replicate the growing leaves
Cathedral spires soar to peal divine inspiration
Skyward hail the rolling sweep of murmuration
As Inca walls stay intact when the Earth heaves

Glories but our exploitations are impossible to ignore
Surely commerce and the environment benefit to meet
For the sake of our poisoned planet I earnestly entreat
Must be mankind within nature's web we answer for

So do we have this desire within to act?
Not while greed is the driver of our race
And we refuse to award nature its place
The edifice of respect will stay cracked
End we must the need to be always in control
Of everything Mother Earth subjected to attack
We need humanity to pause to arrest our track
Of destruction to set harmony as the noble goal

Well Disposed

For we know we can succeed when united
Our peoples have some mighty recent form
During the breathtaking COVID-19 storm
Economic crises many deaths spotlighted
Yet co-operate we did on what had to be done
Minimise our impact on others we most agreed
Mindful of helping those the vulnerable in need
Same mindset to save the third rock from the Sun

I say honour our achievements strive to be upbeat
Admire what the arts and the sciences well conserve
Now set your focus on prizing nature without reserve
The Earth and I need this reverence to stay complete.

An acknowledgement of the strongest bond of all

The primal bond

While mateship is what draws blokes together
Easy female understanding has a wider embrace

Family connections are defined by duty also blood
Sadly they may also provoke guilt or a lasting feud

Yet rising above the fray there is no stronger tie
Than that exists between a mother and her child
No wonder so deep the loss the unrelenting grief
Of a weeping primal wound from this broken bond.

A peon to leading a balanced life, mindful of the self and others

The proper balance

What is it exactly we aim for in our lives?
Happiness or wellbeing come readily to mind
While some may settle simply for satisfaction
Others claim it is rewarding always to be kind

Sad there are those who want to leave their mark
Feel the need to be subjects of perennial fanfare
But surely we owe it to the health of our very selves
Not to rely on the approval of others for our welfare

'Tis doubly important during the COVID-19 pandemic
We best aim to avoid being coerced against our will

Well Disposed

In times when social interaction is so compromised
Self containment becomes the personal goal to instil

For within we do have the resources for resilience
The capacity for curiosity a willingness to explore
To expand our horizons to absorb wonder and beauty
Beckoning - natural, man-made, expanding evermore

To seek the uplifting phrase artwork that inspires
And share with persons of like minded optimism
Yet mindful on our planet which we share with many
That a mark of collective humaneness is altruism

So it seems a mix of checking in and looking out
Is the balance suited best for all of us to aspire
And the onus is on us, yes every single one of us
To know ourselves then reach out others to inspire.

This poem coincided with my preparation for a podcast about the impact of adoption separation on fathers

Upon the loss of a child to adoption

Well the onion layers of my tears
Heavy grief pulsating at the core
The past once lain deeply bound
Thus denial caught in a steely trap
To unburden those hidden years
Buried solitary clogged and raw
Courage has need to be found
First resolve then mount the attack

Relief comes from work done inside
To release the soothing to my pain
Guilt that can no longer be denied
At last the releasing of the shame

My child blesses the mending of the years
Since I peeled away the source of all my tears.

The mini-collection began with me making a booking to have my eyes checked and then imagination took over

Appointments for the senses
[told in five verses]

A visit to the optometrist

I have called and arranged
To visit the optometrist
He said he will see me
I think this is a good start
The appointment is at 9.30
But, I wonder, will I see him?
This remains to be seen.

*****

'Hear, hear!' I say

I have rung the audiologist
I have yet to hear back
I want to make an appointment
I am hoping to hear more.

*****

The wrong specialist

I was not smelling very well
So I tried to make an appointment
To see a rhinologist
He told me I had called the wrong specialist
I replied to him that
I smelled a rat
'You need a special specialist,' he said.

*****

The gentle touch

I had lost my sense of touch
So to cure my deprivation
I saw a specialist in numbness
I found her most consoling
Especially when she told me
She aimed to have me feeling well.

*****

Tasteless

Worried, I rang the ENT specialist
To tell him I did not have good taste

But he laughed at me dismissively
Leaving me with a taste that was bitter
So I decided then and there
This was one appointment
I no longer had any need to keep.

My attempt to get to the bottom of the unresolved railway gauge issue

What were they thinking of?

'Mankind, I have a task for you,' the Omnipotent decreed
'Come up with a system, people and commerce it does impede
Now go away and work on this, I trust you will succeed.'

'Let's make a big mess of this right across the board
Why not multiple gauges, from the narrow to the broad,'
Said the men of wisdom and God's faith was restored.

So spread the railway network, divergence at the very
core
Disagreement about the narrow gauges, there came
to be four
While at the other end, well those Iberians they
went for more.

Theirs the widest between the rails, greater than
Ireland or the Tsar
Yet somehow out of this chaos, one standard gauge
emerged the star
However there remain many irksome breaks and
they resound afar.

Changes of railway gauge delay trade and travel just
as roads do not
Thus we are bound to conclude those pioneers
simply lost the plot
'So now,' says He, still looking on, 'you must put up

with your lot.'

An investigation of the meaning of success, cautioning the reliance upon numbers

Measuring success

There are many definitions of success
But what they all have in common
Is that they should be values based
Centred on goals that are personal
Certainly not the expectations of others
Best to avoid unhelpful comparisons

Aim for a mixture of qualitative
Plus quantitative for balance
Some examples of the former
Are health and relationships
Freedom a sense of fulfilment
Your aim may simply be to live

Well Disposed

Some have a single focus easy for them
They are blessed with a specific talent
Moreover know where and how to apply it
Yet most of us have to toil to succeed

Finally if you measure by numbers
(And this is critically important)
Do not fall into the trap of believing
Money is the only currency of success.

A simple celebration of love

Sent from within

Love is an action
Sent from your heart
A precious word will do

I feel your love
Coming from within
No wonder I treasure you.

The fruitfulness of love is explored

Enough love for three

Your third trimester
Is about to close
What a pity

You say you like
Being pregnant
So I enjoy it too.

It is in my nature
To treasure your body
The fecundity of your shape

Where two hearts are beating
As inside your hemisphere

You nurture our love

A love that began as a seed
And you grew tenderly within
Naturally endures between we two.

A completely different approach, to honour a man who is a joy to watch going about his business

Acrostic accolade

Roger
Outstanding
Graceful
Effortless
Remarkable

Federer
Elegant
Dexterity
Enduring
Reflexes
Elite
Respected

Greatest

Outsmart

Agile

Triumphant

This is a topic that is rarely confronted, even though we all know people who are serial offenders

Overdue

Your being late
Be it for a meeting
Or goodness me a date
Shows rank lack of respect
For every other person involved

By being unpunctual
You convey selfishness
In thought and in the actual
Not how you would treat your mother
So please respect all of us by being on time.

The shortened match playing times in 2020 brought this issue to a head

The decline of Australian football

What a pity that as a spectacle the AFL has very much declined
Aiming to kick a winning tally is outmoded some say maligned
For today the overall goal is to restrict the opponent's score
(Oh for when the grand final totalled 300 points and more)

Remember when coaching was about creating time and space
Instead we have turnovers and stoppages blocking their place
As well as zoning, the flood and such overuse of

handball
Not the open game founders of the rules had in mind at all

Imagine what would happen if the game reverted to attack
Those ugly close in tussles associated with the player pack
Would disappear replaced by long kicks aerial contests galore
As well as goals aplenty; I say banish this defensive eyesore!

I have long wondered about these gender word pairings – are they coincidental?

The words have it

Consider the genders in our human choir
True **man** is the shortening of **woman**
As **male** is a diminutive of **female**
Proof etymology has spoken
Ladies are the more entire.

There has long been discussion about the meaning and sudden ending of the poem ***'Kubla Khan'***

What Coleridge had in mind

The poem *Kubla Khan* by Coleridge
Has been declared a fantasy
Exotic or replace the x with an r
Why the critics cannot agree

References to the 'pleasure dome'
'Sinuous rills' 'fertile ground'
'That deep romantic chasm'
Among images that confound

'For he on honey-dew hath fed
And drunk the milk of paradise'
Is abruptly how this poem ends

The person from Porlock device

Some have said that the flow of ideas
From Coleridge simply ebbed to a drought
Others are still heard to wish that Porlock
Be used today to give more writers an out

Whatever your take on his Xanadu
Published or the symbolism behind
You've become part of the debate
About what Coleridge had in mind.

Some fun touring the oceans

Island play

If Fiji connects to feijoa
As Samoa does to samosa
Surely Mauritius is delicious

Just as Tahiti is made to relate to treaty
So Seychelles are on the seashore
But yet nothing matches Tonga.

At the end of 2020, it is time to look back upon our experiences in the state of Victoria

Coronavirus reflections

During the pandemic we've learned new words and
phrases
Relating to lockdowns, waves, steps, stages and even
phases

Staying apart keeps us together when translated
Means *We're all in this together* although isolated

COVID tests need long queues a probe deep up the
nose
Meant to measure the active cases, tho' some did
oppose
Social distancing and eventually having to wear a

mask
For the conspiracy theory crackpots just too much to ask

Panic buying of trolley loads of pasta flour mince and toilet paper
Surely not a product of the restaurant meal home delivery caper?

Hand sanitiser that not only kills the virus but also our hands
Until after the curve is flattened we cannot watch live bands

Your principal place of residence you had to nominate
Because no more escaping to the beach or country estate
Restrictions resulting from clusters and city

hotspots
Hard borders imposed, separated families hurting lots

Multiple deaths in aged care definitely not bad luck
Saw state and federal leaders each passing the buck

Workers laid off, even with *Jobkeeper,* so compromising wealth
Uncertainty, not abetted by *Jobseeker*, undermines mental health

Sydney *Ruby Princess* fiasco then proclaimed gold standard
Victorian numbers soared the state became adversely branded
Then as an outcome of the bungled hotel quarantine
Your supermarket stays closed for another deep clean

Home schooling difficult for parents working from
home
Children without classroom discipline a tendency
to roam

Ring fencing suburbs you rediscovered your
postcode
Then found the road map out did not refer to your
road

Melburnians dare break the curfew or you will be
in trouble
On the way out you must choose but one household
bubble

The city surrounded by a ring of steel with
associated heavy fines
For those who dare to breach the cordon defying

strict guidelines

If you're confused by the many changes that affect the rules
You are not alone across households, businesses and schools
Yet compared to America where denial does preside
Glad that it is safe Australia where we choose to reside.

The Ripple Effect

This, a shape poem, needs no further explanation

Helicopter seeds

The sycamore seed

released

from

the parent

tree

falls

spinning

Well Disposed

helicopter-like

spiralling

on the breeze

aiming to land

in the loam

away

from the canopy

and then

twirling

airborne

freedom lost

the seed

settles . . .

and

germinates.

I was inspired by weathered ladder, still in excellent condition, leaning against the wall at a friend's house

In praise of wooden ladders

Give me a bespoke wooden ladder
Of sturdy rungs and rails
Then I will paint your timber walls
And climb extended to the roof

Always secure in the knowledge
That it is neither moulded metal
(And therefore conductor free)
Nor made in China under duress.

At the destination airport we all have congregated around the carousel . . .

At the baggage claim

See an assembly of suitcases
Slide lapping on the conveyor
Anticipating there is a match
For each passenger who waits

Finally when they all
Have been claimed
There are a few left behind
This clustering of orphans

Which means either
Bags have been wrongly taken
And your one has flown

Or maybe it is on another flight!

The vagaries of English provide a deep well of material ...

Janus words

There is a class of words
Confusing to say the least
Because the same spelling
Can mean the very opposite
Oh English can be a beast.

Take dust as an example
To cover with fine specks
As in dusting a crop
But also to brush clean
Subject of household checks

Cleanliness is an objective

Well Disposed

That busy people may shun
So it becomes overlooked
Best to overlook the task
To make sure it is done

And when the job is through
No mess remains behind
Nothing to clean up is left
As the cleaner gets to leave
So is another contranym defined

There is one final word
That displays cause and effect
A boat is said to withstand a storm
But the same event will wear rocks away
Yet the opposed variants of weather are correct!

These a few of the words
That are two-faced

Like the first month
Of every calendar year
There you have the taste.

I could not resist having some fun with people who can be manipulated

Celebrating Alec Guinness

Setting:

In the Anagram Hall of Fame, there are standout celebrities whose names offer playful options. However beware of loopy lies, for example ELVIS LIVES.

Authentically, athletically:

From his ABLUTIONS *USAIN BOLT* emerges mighty fast

Meanwhile MILLIONS SEE *LIONEL MESSI* scoring goals.

Musically:

ERIC CLAPTON admits he is tired of being *NARCOLEPTIC* as

PRESBYTERIANS have been converted to *BRITNEY SPEARS*.

On the screen:

We know STEVE IRWIN crossed easily to *INTERVIEWS*

And CLINT EASTWOOD embodies *OLD WEST ACTION*

As MARTIN SCORSESE encourages *MINOR ACTRESSES*

So MEG RYAN is transformed split out of *GERMANY*.

Culminating in the UK:

MARGARET THATCHER reincarnates as *THAT GREAT CHARMER*

Whereas her compatriot THERESA MAY invites all
to *SHARE MY TEA*
Still ALEC GUINNESS is the ultimate because he
owns *GENUINE CLASS.*

I was drawn to explore an oft-used opening line, this time in an adoption context

Love and adoption

Come speak to me of love
And I will show you
Families forced apart by adoption

First there is the father
Not about to provide support
For the woman he adored (he said)

Fundamentally . . . this is where the adoption begins

Turn to the mother caught in a bind

Well Disposed

Agonising about the welfare of her infant
Destined never to forget her grievous loss

Placed is the adopted person
Cared for by a family of strangers
Pondering if and where they belong

Children were too young to have their say

So speak to me of love
And I will tell you
About the heartbreak called adoption

Save today we are more enlightened
And adoption has come to be seen
As the option of last resort

Mercifully!

The trigger here was an article about the epidemic of shame that compromises our emotional awareness

Mindful

There are many dozens of emotions
Yet most of us can name only three
Simply put they are glad, sad and mad
Almost unspoken is the epidemic of feeling bad
The shame accrued from both you and me
Contempt at the core of unloving notions
So retarding the development of personal potential
Meaning to own a well-rounded emotional vocabulary
Grounded by empathy and understanding ranks as essential.

A reality of post-adoption matters is exposed

The shuttered men

Adoption is often perceived
To be solely women's business
Which is by no means accurate
Because men are affected too

Truly both male and female
Adopted persons are dislocated
And don't forget the fathers
Who grieve for their lost child

But men are heard from
Generally rather less often
For many a product of being
Less connected with their feelings

Then others acutely aware of
The remarked gender imbalance
Stay safely in the background
Until invited to have their say

Let us realise any opportunities
For these men who have suffered
The impact of adoption separation
To add their voices to the conversation
And help expose the present shuttered view.

This trio of poems began as separate entities, until I realised they formed a progression

Outward bound

Thanks to the printing press

Mark me a place called Nirvana
I aim to go there whenever I can
The words are what attract me
From writers writing with elan

Some leave enough to the imagination
Because the visual is not spoon fed
Much to engage the willing reader
Aim to stimulate the heart and head

Other authors describe a vivid scene
Impressions are conveyed with style
Seek to capture then hold our interest
They set aside our troubles for a while

Books have brought joy to plenty
Since the advent of the printing press
They have broadened many minds
Here is one fan I am bound to confess.

*****

Wanderlust

Books can serve as the appetiser
To the main course in your hands alone
You need find the necessary components
Bound to take you away from home.

Well Disposed

Put on your long-distance glasses
Also you will need a close-up pair
To seek the small alongside the big
You are aiming for a balanced fare.

May your searching be extensive
Maybe you hope it will never cease
Let the wanderlust go grab you
Top of the menu for personal peace.

Somewhere in your journey
So there might come a time
When all the ingredients blend
Add to the meaning of sublime.

Now go buy your freedom ticket
For what is there to lose
Surely it has to be exploration
The key for the life you choose.

*****

Stimulation beyond

Down stultified and apathetic
Go seek stimulation beyond
This self-absorbed residency
So take the effort to respond
Undermine just staying stuck.

Rather explore big horizons
What lies tipping over the rim
The tantalising surely beckons
New places pursued to the brim
Allow hearts and minds to grow.

Set aside material impedimenta
Do cast a stone into every pond

Go follow the ripples so created and
Ride waves of stimulation way beyond
Those stay-at-homes you left behind.

This began at a chance encounter, whilst with my grandson, with the euphonious pardalote

Animal tales

'I know I shall miss you'
Said the pardalote to the stoat.
'I do not plan to go anywhere,'
Replied the dweller of the den, pausing,
'You as a bird I find to be absurd.'

'Where is it you are buzzing?'
Said the beaver to the bee.
'Oh everywhere in particular,
For when the nectar is sparse
It's a believer I have to be.'

At the great kennel, from poodle to malamute

Well Disposed

Other motley canines ranging solo to the pack
Stands out one breed, barker of the truth.
For says the greyhound, eyes on the track,
'There (I cannot deny) for the race of dog go I.'

'Let me give you some sage advice
(People come fishing all the time),'
Said no dill Rosemary to holy Basil,
'While some rivers may be past their prime
This one is about giving you the benefit of the trout.'

The tree that sighs and connects you to the land is deserving of its own poem

The conversation tree

Fine native tree of Australia
Resplendent in droopy foliage
Cassowary feathers come to mind

Plenty of native birds gather
From my female seeded cones
Food and propagation are assured

Suitable conditions are
Saline and prone to drought
Indeed my distribution is wide

Ideal for our desert climate

I lose little water to the air
And so am self-contained

Prone to depletion by fire
I draw nutrients from my ashes
Hail resurrect another phoenix tree

Renowned for self-mulching
I add to the soil underneath
Simple conservation guaranteed

I am an aeolian harp keening
Via thousands of fine filaments
Secrets that unfold upon the breeze

Now you have attended to this message
Please go pollinate my many virtues
I be casuarina also known as she-oak.

The other great challenge of our times seemed to be set aside during the pandemic

Careless custodians

Self-appointed custodians of this planet Earth
Somehow over history we have become divided
Into the rapacious, the oblivious and the protective
Dominance of the first two has left a world lopsided

The constant human imperative to conquer nature
So many species and habitats are now under threat
Planned obsolescence and the resultant waste means
Climate action targets are set aside or pass by un-met

Reckless exploitation of resources mineral and plant
Via manufacturing that corrupts the water and the air

Well Disposed

Today the health of our planet and its populations
Are compromised little do many leaders frankly care

So it is up to the protectors to generate a groundswell
Led by the young who stand to inherit the mighty mess
Bequeathed by the profligate and their flagrant inaction
Mother Earth is bound to wish the intrepid every success.

I wrote this after listening to the commentary resulting from the international climate conference in Glasgow

Coal(ition)

'Let's preserve the 'coal' in Coalition,'
Said Barnaby being his most disarmed
'COP 26 targets mean absolutely nothing
When the world revolves on supply and demand.'

'If countries overseas need Australian coal
Then thanks to us they will get plenty sent
Further we will dig more and bigger mines
To keep the jobs of every falling one percent.'

'It's all about employment,' said Scomo Aussie PM,
'To save the traditional economy indeed keep it kicking;

Of course our plans mean the Earth will stay in good
shape.'
(In no way due to Canberra's shameless politicking.)

How is it that Australian governments local and state
Have set emission targets they intend fully to meet
Yet for our children the federal Coalition refuses to
commit?
Time to hark the leadership from boardroom, land and
street.

For overall the population is clear about the necessity
To phase out fossil fuels in favour of sun and wind
Opportunities that redefine what is to be the future
And save this our planet – surely the ultimate win-
win.

When, in October 2021, the restrictions were eased, a group of us ventured to the northeast corner of Victoria

Beyond Tallangatta (in the Upper Murray) . . .

If you carry on to Corryong there you will belong
To tales in the bar about the exploits of Jack Riley
He of Banjo's famous ride for every pulsating stride
Sure enough this poet Paterson is rated very highly.

Yet *The Man from Snowy River* has more to deliver
Adapted twice from the page on to the big screen
And so the legend grows as his local statue shows
Of the town attractions this has to be the most seen.

There is another versifier spoke around the campfire
Our CJ Dennis is as Australian as any poet might be

He wrote of *Corryong* like there uplifted and on song
Before to music here was born a Kernaghan named
Lee.

So when you go to Corryong in the Shire of Towong
Be prepared to be surrounded by history and rhyme
Encircled by hills that promise pleasure and thrills
And people bound to guarantee you a cracking time.

Another road trip, this time interstate, took us to the far west of New South Wales

The hill once broken

Here is a hill no longer there
For it is a hill that was broken
Leaving a legacy of mullock heaps
Denuded and upraised as a token

To the mining of lead and zinc
A discovery precious metal too
This dirty backdrop to the Silver City
Natural it's where the Trade Unions grew

For underground was a dying hell back then
Yet today upon the waste all the dead are recorded
While over the city we know as Broken Hill

Finally first heritage status has been accorded

When you venture to view the architecture most
splendid
You may be moved to proclaim this olden Hill has
mended.

This happened to me and remains a mystery; the outcome is my best guess

Family heirloom

Once I had a ring
Suddenly it wasn't there
Horseshoed on my finger
Was but the shank
Yet of the shoulder
Head and stone
Well they had disappeared

Where I first noticed
My hand felt different
I searched carpet and chair
Then I retraced my steps homewards
The severed bits were not to be found

So at $2000 an ounce I guess
A lucky street walker has struck gold.

The inspiration here is the hobby of a friend

Ode to model trains

Model trains have long appealed across the ages
Serb and Croat look on the same side of the tracks
Even when they do locomote on different gauges.

Some thrive on rail talk spread across the nations
While others choose to keep the fun closer to home
Yet common is the rush from trains going by stations.

Be it creative design making scenery of your own
Or solving electronic problems helped by the savvy
Multi-generational relationships are likely to be sown.

So when you have the room and your time is up for sale

You are ready to minituarise a fantasy of your youth
And enjoy those tracks and trains now on another
scale.

Some people are obsessed with supreme achievements; indeed there is a well known book about world records published annually

Citius, Altius, Fortius - Communiter

Wherein lies any link between
The personal quest to outdo
And a dazzled admiration
Of achievement pinnacles
Especially the record-holders
The fastest highest strongest
Overall the biggest and the best
Our idol has become giantism?

Seen as mindless aspiration
Is but one interpretation
Fated for a personal fall
But replace push with the pull

And a glass that is half full
Then the sage may come to stand tall.

Pause where is it
Exactly do you fit
Plead anywhere but the pit
Of endless mediocrity
An unfulfilled wannabee
Captive to a life of monotony?

Surely it is better to have tried
And abjectly failed
Than to not even tried at all.

For the sake of our good health
It is better those records so set
Remain as background appreciation
Rather than be the primary fixation.

To put these attainments into perspective
'Tis not purely magnitude that is paramount
Instead it is what lies behind their very making
Together skill and attitude deserve account.

In sum do not dwell vicariously on that attained without
But instead always attend to what you can control within.

This quatrain was precipitated by the idle question, 'Was a butterfly formerly known as a flutterby?' (The answer is 'No.')

Naturally Spooner

When you espy the butterfly flutter by
Catch the woodpecker pecker wood
Then descry the flycatcher catch a fly
Only your first sighting is Spooner good.

In February 2022, when the COVID induced restrictions started to lift, a group of us decided to go over the seas for a holiday . . .

Positively Norfolk Island

It was James Commander Cook
Who found and then named
Pine rich Norfolk Island
A dot in his vast Pacific realm

He reported back to his superiors
Here was timber for naval masts
Plans for Norfolk Island
Need to keep the French at bay

Roll on a mere fourteen years
Arrives the First Fleet overflow
Penal Norfolk Island

Man's inhumanity to man

Escape proof and remote
So far from prying eyes
Punishing Norfolk Island
For nigh on sixty years

Then a plea to Victoria on the throne
From overcrowded Pitcairn far away
Protective Norfolk Island
For descendants of the *Bounty* mutineers

When as a visitor you arrive upon the isle
You will be surrounded by this history
Proudly Norfolk Island
Eight Pitcairn families to the fore

The island is a living museum
Tourism reinforces this fact

Pause on Norfolk Island
For there is more bound to appeal

The weather here is most benign
It's not too hot and never cold
Pine for Norfolk Island
Temperate throughout the year

The lifestyle is very laid back
The service is at best relaxed
Pacific Norfolk Island
Removed from mainland hustle

To bring about a smile
The telephone book is a must
Portrait of Norfolk Island
Nicknames make the list

Supermarket prices are extravagant

Yet eating out prices do not shock
Paradoxical Norfolk Island
Surely that's part of its charm

The only settlement in the isle centre
Is surrounded by cattle grids
Practical Norfolk Island
Curbs bovines to its country roads

Remoteness is still a virtue
In the eyes of many locals
Promoting Norfolk Island
Ensures their culture remains intact

Which is why extending the jetty
To build the obvious deep water
Port for Norfolk Island
Has many shaking their heads

Well Disposed

The island is administered by Australia but
Locals would prefer to run their own affairs
Paramount for Norfolk Island
The people demand to be heard

Whilst the islanders welcome their visitors
Please come in numbers that do not overwhelm
Possessive Norfolk Island
Is intent on keeping Australia at bay.

The events that unfolded in 2021 meant a postscript to 2020 was surely called for (this was written in September 2021, the month the Chief Health Officer of Victoria, Professor Brett Sutton, sagely proclaimed: Getting tested does not make you positive. Getting infected is what makes you positive*)*

Groundhog year

As we turned over the calendar to 2021
We hoped we had left 2020 well behind
But this was not to be we discovered as
The new year began COVIDly to unwind

There arose matters that stole our attention
When two deadly factors began to emerge
The bungling of the promised vaccine rollout
Supplied the alarming Delta variant surge

Into our lexicon new phrases began to appear

'Infectious in the community', 'locally acquired'
As fresh 'exposure sites' were listed every day
Promoting snap lockdowns that barely expired

Businesses struggled to keep themselves alive
Plans to stay open at the mercy of virus spread
From customers and staff, delivery drivers too
Impossible to predict what closures lay ahead

Epidemiologists at last found they had a niche
And praise to those policing our many borders
There to check the flow of goods and people
And arrest those breaching public health orders

We were told the non-compliant risked starting
A 'super-spreader event' so best stay at home
Cancel your travel plans let the credits accrue
Lock up your passport defer that foreign roam

Across the year we heard constant exhortations
'Don't forget to QR code' wherever you shop
'Line up for the jab' ignore the confusing advice
Rules plus vaccination will give COVID* the chop

While 2021 seems like an extension of last year
Surely a return to freedom we are overdue
So from behind my mask I do exhort
Forever optimistic bring on 2022.

* Perhaps COVID can be redefined as *Concerning Outbreak Variant Is Delta*?

*I wrote this when the active case numbers in New South Wales and Victoria were disturbingly high and the professional health advice showed signs of being downgraded; the inspiration for the poem came from the Epilogue of '**Into the Rip**', a book by Damien Cave*

Perspective

I'd hate to be the one to let everybody down
By not wearing a mask when the experts said
It is a means of keeping COVID-19 at bay
And helps the wearers not add to the dead.

I would not want to be the haphazard one
Who neglected to QR code at the supermarket
Making life difficult for the contact tracers
Better all round I make myself an easy target.

Spare me the embarrassment of opening my home

Well Disposed

When the health rules proclaim this is forbidden
Enclosed gatherings represent the greatest risk
Where Delta enters and leaves the house unbidden.

Enough of the me less I be regarded self-centred
When clear we need to beat this pandemic united
Two years of compliance for the common good
The overture to 2022 when lost freedoms reignited.

'I'd hate to be the one who let everybody down'
Is what a soldier may have said in World War Two
Let us not forget that on the battlefield and at home
Isolated for six years is what our forebears went through.

This was written in mid-2021, before Victoria's final surge

Lockdown Gold Medals awarded to Australian States (henceforth known as the **Lockies**):

Frequency = VICTORIA

Permanency = WESTERN AUSTRALIA

Brevity = SOUTH AUSTRALIA

The Steven Bradbury Special Award for Coming from Last to First with Minimum Effort * = NEW SOUTH WALES

* (aka the Tarnished Gold Standard)

The Way Ahead

Volunteering at the Visitor Centre

Volunteering is
Giving back to
The community
In spirit
And in kind
What has been
Given to us
And others
Many times.

For all those volunteers
Serving visitors in our town
Information is their currency
With an attitude of helping

At the heart of what they give

Now and then in return
Yes volunteered to them
'Thank you' says the visitor
The unsolicited bonus
Of their service giving back.

My clever travelling sprinkler

My intrepid travelling sprinkler
Is like a tractor on the lawn
No driver at the throttle.

My guided travelling sprinkler
Takes the snaking route ahead
And pulls its trail behind.

My wetted travelling sprinkler
Spreads the liquid bounty from
The hose it does bestride.

My clever travelling sprinkler
Tracks the water to its source
Then turns off the tap.

Mrs Dutton's leg (a tale of separation spread over two locations)

'The leg of Mrs Dutton'
Is what the gravesite says
1865 the date of interment
But the rest of Mrs Dutton
Whereabouts her final plot?

It is in another town
At a cemetery remote
Online records tell us
Also Mrs Dutton lived
Nigh another fifty years.

How the loss occurred

There are no facts on this
Was she run over by a heavy dray
Or perhaps hobbled by gangrene
What caused her leg to go?

Mrs Dutton would have been
Just forty-two at the time
Awaiting daughter number four
Child the last one of eight
Who was born in '66.

Perhaps the oldest daughter stayed
On to help with daily chores
Maybe Mr Dutton made a crutch
Then again a wooden leg
To ease the burden for his wife.

Leaving a memorial for a leg
May seem a might peculiar

There is no Christian protocol
That decrees a severed limb
Must lie in sacred ground.

But a famous precedent does exist
From the US Civil War no less
Stonewall Jackson's severed arm
Has a headstone all to itself
Did Mrs Dutton ever know?

Truly there are gaps aplenty
In the tale of Mrs Dutton's leg
Beyond birth death and marriage
Conjecture is destined to exist
Thus alternatives are allowed.

To make Mrs Dutton die intact
And alleviate her distress
I want the inscription to be wrong

The impish mason meant to write
'Here lies a leg of mutton'!

Why the local mason
Would deign to mark a grave
For a piece of sheep
Is a completely different story
That's for someone else to tell.

Avenues of Honour

One hundred years ago . . .

An empire under threat
The quest for adventure
Is why they volunteered
To fight in World War One

Within our country lay
Respect for the enlisted
Knitting for the troops
A grateful welcome home

But it is what came after
The reminder that dwells

Well Disposed

Countless war memorials
A legacy of the horrors
And very much Australian
Abundant Avenues of Honour

Tributes in tree and plaque
For locals who signed on
To serve and many perish
In places far from home

It is those who fought away
Not the dying in the course
That the Avenues acclaim
The value of giving settled
While the sacrifice was theirs
Surely the honouring be ours

The boulevards remain
Tidy and preserved

A century of marking
Those who served us well

These Avenues of Honour
Standing in the present
Mark a time in history
When the population
Considered it a privilege
For men and women
To stand for this Australia
In the name of deterring
Threats of aggression to
The integrity of our shores

Rarely have those
Who fought for us
In conflicts overseas
Been as well regarded
From coast to coast

Both during and after
As the service men
And service women
Who were deployed
Across the Great War

How have we changed.

Both hands

Right is right and left is wrong
For our language tells us so
Using words that best belong
In languages we no longer know.

Sinister is dark and from the left
Dexterous is so accomplished right
Gauche means clumsy it is the left
Adroit of course rewards the right.

Bias is embedded in the split
And left does not fare too well
Comes the time we must admit
That right is not bound to excel.

Well Disposed

A proper balance our perception aim
Left and right weighted just the same.

So we must cast out all left-handed blight
Then each hand is neither wrong nor right.

The cracks in the ceiling

I peer at the cracks above me
The ceiling they adorn
I begin to imagine
Places far away

For every trace beckons me
Each crooked plaster line
A road to the horizon
Promise of beyond

I am standing in a Parisian gallery
Impressionists on every wall
Their brilliance so intense
I regret I must move on

To the Yangtze before the gorges flood
An artery of a nation large and full
Busy people dominate the scene
I hanker for pristine ground

I find Chicken deep in Alaska
Can say I have been there
Off the beaten track
I want to explore

An isolated crack to South Georgia
And Ernest Shackleton's grave
The bitter howling winds
I shiver for some heat

Calls the Atacama by the ceiling rose
So warm most of the year round
Any talk of sparing moisture
Simply highlights the gap

Well Disposed

Lying along the cornice boundary
It's where the water seeps in
Like on squelchy beaches
Mud between the toes

Takes me to the Bay of Fundy
And the tide is rushing in
Each wave an advance
Water is chasing me

Underneath the mighty waterfall
Iguazu is where I'm now at
But soaked to the skin
I need to get away

So I seek another line to the corner
The farthest from my repose
Yet I'm in outer space

Jupiter it has to be

For now that's the end of my tether
I need a break closer to home
The family is my anchor
And it is to you I turn

Please delay repair this bedroom ceiling
In my mind it's the pathway to outside
Because as long I remain bedridden
These cracks are my sole escape.

Germs

Germs they have a gender
Since Marsha told me so
When she fell ill last night
The he-germs inside of her
Oh they did cop a serve
Then I asked about the she
They go after men she said
I thought I'd think it through.

Is he within the she
And her within the him
Exclusively
Or could they roam about
He and she to both
Randomly?

Why not I say it could be fun
And think about the times
When he and she are in the him
Or her, multiplying frantically
But the morals of such germs
These we must a-medicate
If they have their way with us
Then we're confined to bed.

Yet there is another take
On gender germy things
Examine next she within the her
Then also he inside the him
'Tis simply not the same
For they are at one alike
So sickness cannot come
The germs and we are bored
Life is on an even plane

And where's the fun in that?

So it is best we do believe
What Marsha said was true
He must be inside of her
And . . . she pursuing him.

The right track

When I was wandering in the bush
I reached a fork that cleft the track
There was no sign at this point
Which showed me where to go
But I knew I could not go back.

Because to return to the south
Meant a retreat to what had been
I was looking for a way ahead
To explore fresh avenues and
Welcome a change of scene.

So I stood there at the split
Uncertain where to go forth
The lower trail beckoned me

Also the right ascending path
For each was bearing north.

Far as I could tell from there
Both of them appealed to me
At the dividing point between
My troubled past and
Where I desired to be.

I made my camp near the fork
Determined what I must do
Not knowing which to prefer
I aimed to try both the tracks
To accept what would ensue.

An open mind was new for me
In my tent a makeshift base
Sleeping well at night I knew
Would set my daytime course

Well Disposed

I felt the promise of this place.

When next morning I set out
On the rightmost fainter route
I found I followed it with ease
Through aspects most serene
It seemed this trail could suit.

But just to make sure of this
I walked the other grade
But it deviated from the north
West to a lookout facing south
This way forth was paid.

I had an easy sleep that night
Well protected inside my tent
Close I leave this place alone
Drawn to a most alluring trail
At this juncture I felt content.

Well Disposed

My shelter I decamped next dawn
Intent upon the dexter track
Whereon my course was fixed
So adroit my split decision
I have never looked back.

Love is on the rails

A man deprived of love is
Like a loco missing steam
Stalled empty at the station
For a train without a soul
Means that he is absent too.

Love is at the heart of
What gives us joy and thrill
But take away the fire
Means life has lost its kick
We lay idle off the track.

Yet light those firebox coals
See that engine steam away
Boisterously tender in behind

Now the signals are all clear
On the line to Destiny and Hope.

When love is full steam ahead
Then his and her tracks do
Converge at all the points
The common ties their bond
And two loving souls are one.

The song within my heart

Come let us speak of love
For I know you are a fan
Fire below and stars above
These are within the span
Of joy possible on Earth
Each song inside our heart
The vision of our birth
Either together or apart
Our songs are truly one
So be it the cool of night
Or beneath the warming sun
Harmony is our inner light.

Through song as in verse
Words of love shall flow

Well Disposed

In these phrases we immerse
'I cannot let you go
You are every breath I take
The purpose in my life
Why each day I want awake'
You are my cure to the strife
That is this planet's lot
Desire I cast such gloom aside
To focus on your spot
The love you glow inside.

You and only you it is true
Are the song within my heart.

Rhombus 2

I
am a
mineral
made of carbon
born deep inside the Earth
before I was heated, pressured and
impelled to near the surface
in kimberlitic pipes
so becoming
a gem
I
am a
precious
jewellery stone
that every woman covets

all my facets 58
Diamond
I am
1

Most of all

I want to be the dates you fold into your spicy dishes
The brandy balls you roll between your palms
I want to be the forget-me-nots you plant
And tend with touching care.

I want to be your solar panels you'll never be without
Then I am the hot water that always runs for you
I want to be the shoes you slip into with ease
We can walk forever tied.

I want to be the list you make to start the day
Firmly there on top is where I'd like to be
I want to be the route map of your trips
I'm moving along with you.

Well Disposed

I want to be every loving thought of yours yet
Most of all I want to belong deep inside your heart.

Catch-2022
(A non-poetic endpiece)

In January 2022, for the umpteenth time I re-read ***Catch-22***, Joseph Heller's masterpiece. I discovered it to be the perfect entertainment for the latter phases of the COVID pandemic; there are multiple, delicious parallels of paradox and mistiming. These are recorded in the present tense below:

- When we are told *we're all in this together* this means every individual must isolate

- When vaccines are advanced as the way out of the immediate crisis, they are not available

- When rapid antigen tests are touted as the means of relieving pressure on PCR testing, they are impossible for most in the community to source

- When, as Omicron rages, reassuring guidance on public health and financial assistance become the most needed, governments are nigh invisible

- When COVID contagion risk is the greatest, mandated restrictions on our movements are the least

- When, during the Omicron surge governments best be in credulity credit, they find themselves in debt.

Let it go,
Let it out,
Let it all unravel,
Let it free
And it will be
A path on which to travel.

Michael Leunig

Cover design by **GenesisFX**, *Ballan, Victoria*

www.ingramcontent.com/pod-product-compliance
Lightning Source LLC
Chambersburg PA
CBHW060525090426
42735CB00011B/2370
9781922270856